Holidays and Entertainments

By Barbara Brooks and Richard Whittingham
Illustrated by Joe Rogers

Created by SYSTEMS FOR EDUCATION, Inc., *Chicago*
Published by THE SOUTHWESTERN COMPANY., *Nashville*

CONTENTS

AMERICAN HOLIDAYS

HOLIDAYS THROUGHOUT THE WORLD

8

PARTIES and ENTERTAINING

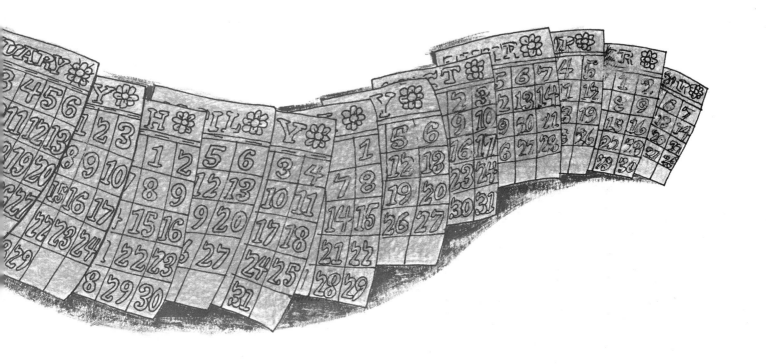

American Holidays

New Year's Day

THE CLOCK IS ABOUT TO STRIKE midnight. It is New Year's Eve. In New York hundreds of thousands of people have jammed into Times Square—the center of the city—to welcome the new year. The last seconds of the old year tick away. When 12 o'clock arrives, a great cheer goes up, horns blow, firecrackers explode, and people sing "Should old acquaintance be forgot, and days of auld lang syne." It is now January 1st, the beginning of a new year.

New Year's Day is the world's birthday. It is celebrated in almost every country in the world. It is a day to look back over the past year and remember all the good things that have happened. It is a time to look back at mistakes, and to make "resolutions" to avoid these mistakes in the new year.

People celebrate New Year's Day in different ways throughout the world. In England and Scotland, large bonfires are built. In France, gifts are exchanged on New Year's Day. In some countries children go from door to door to receive cookies and cakes.

Perhaps the most popular custom throughout the world is going visiting. People in many parts of the world open their doors to greet their friends and neighbors on New Year's Day. Cookies, candies, nuts, cakes, and other good things are offered at each house. This friendly custom began in China many years ago.

There have been some strange customs on New Year's Day. They are *superstitions*. That is, they are strange ideas people believed even though there was no real reason to believe them. That a rabbit's foot brings good luck or that breaking a mirror brings seven years bad luck are superstitions.

The most famous superstition for New Year's Day is called "first footing." People in many European countries believed that the first visitor who entered their house on New Year's Day would bring either good luck or bad luck for the whole year. A dark-haired man would bring good luck. A woman or a man with light hair would bring bad luck. So, to be on the safe side, some towns chose a man with dark hair to go quickly from house to house. After he made his rounds, the houses would be open to other visitors.

In Japan, women placed beans on the floor in the four corners of the house. This was supposed to drive evil spirits from the house for the new year.

In the United States the new year is celebrated with New Year's Eve parties, paper hats, noise, music, and good friendship. Parades are also an important part of the celebration.

The "Mummers" parade on January 1st each year in Philadelphia, Pennsylvania, is one of the biggest parades in the world. A "mummer" is a man who wears a mask or costume. The Philadelphia parade lasts 10 hours, and is said to cost over one million dollars. The leader of the parade is called "King Momus," and is dressed in a brightly colored costume. He is followed by a long line of magnificent floats, each one different, and specially decorated for the occasion. There are marching bands. The men in the parade

are dressed as clowns, animals, historical figures, and even women (because no women are allowed in the parade). The costumes are gay and colorful, and many are covered with flowers, baubles, sequins, and jewelry.

On the other coast of the United States in Pasadena, California, is another famous parade — the Tournament of Roses. A "queen" leads the parade. Millions of flowers, especially roses, decorate the floats. It is one of the most beautiful parades in the world. The climax of the pageant is the Rose Bowl football game.

Everyone, however, does not celebrate the new year on January 1st. The date of the new year depends on the calendar that is used. In the past, different days have been New Year's Day because of the different calendars that were used. Even today, some countries or groups of people celebrate according to other calendars.

The wonderful thing about New Year's — whenever it occurs — is that a whole new year lies ahead. The sad thing is that another year has passed.

Lincoln's Birthday

ABRAHAM LINCOLN WAS BORN February 12, 1809. He became the 16th president of the United States, and one of the most famous men in our history. Each year we honor the birthday of this great man.

In the woods of Kentucky where Abraham Lincoln was born, the people were very poor. The men were farmers or tradesmen who worked long and hard each day to earn enough to support their families. The

Lincoln family was no different. Abraham was born in a small log cabin. His parents could not read or write. There were no schools nearby. Abraham Lincoln spent at most only one year in school, but he learned to read and write.

The Lincoln family moved to Indiana, and later to Illinois. As a young man, Abraham left home to live in New Salem, Illinois. He worked at various odd jobs, and studied in his spare time. Finally, he entered politics and was elected to the Illinois state assembly. He continued to study. In time he became a lawyer.

He was elected to the United States Congress, but served only one two-year term. He later tried for the Senate. His opponent was Senator Stephen Douglas. Lincoln lost that election, but two years later, in 1860, he ran again against Douglas. This time the two men were running for the presidency of the United States. This time Lincoln won the election.

Shortly after his election, the Civil War broke out. Abraham Lincoln found himself as president in the most difficult years our nation has ever faced.

In 1863, Lincoln bravely met the problem of slavery. He issued the Emancipation Proclamation which freed the slaves.

The Civil War still raged. Abraham Lincoln struggled to bring the nation back together. After four bitter years of fighting, the war ended on April 9, 1865. The United States was again united as one nation.

Five days later, Abraham Lincoln went with his wife to Ford's Theater in Washington, D.C., to watch a play. There he was shot to death by John Wilkes Booth.

The world would not forget this great man. He is remembered each year on February 12th for preserving the country in its most tragic hours. He is honored for the strength and courage he displayed in defending the rights of all men as equal. And he is admired for the wonderful example he left to us of rising through hard work, determination, and skill to the highest office in the United States.

Washington's Birthday

WASHINGTON, D.C., the state of Washington, the Washington Monument, the George Washington Bridge —almost everywhere in the United States there is something named after George Washington. He is America's most famous leader, called the "Father of His Country."

It is only proper that we honor Washington's birthday as a holiday. George Washington was a great general who led our army against the British in our war of independence, the Revolutionary War. He defeated the British forces, and America became a new, free nation.

After the war, in 1789, George Washington was elected the first president of the United States. He served for eight years. Washington helped to establish our Constitution, and helped build a new and orderly government. He provided the foundation so the United States could grow into a great nation.

Washington's birthday is celebrated on the third Monday in February. He was born February 11, 1732. The

calendar was changed 20 years later and his birthday became February 22. Unlike Abraham Lincoln, George Washington was born of fairly wealthy parents in Virginia. At 16, he went to live at Mount Vernon, a beautiful home on the Potomac River in Alexandria, Virginia. This was to be his home for the rest of his life. It is there that Washington is buried. Today, Mount Vernon is one of the most famous landmarks in the United States.

The first celebration of Washington's birthday was in 1781. It was a great honor, because Washington was still alive. Troops marched in the streets, and the day was made a holiday. Very few men in history have received such an honor in their lifetime.

Today, Washington's birthday is celebrated with cherry pies and talk of little boys chopping down cherry trees. In schools throughout the United States, children read and write stories about his wonderful deeds.

George Washington did not chop down a cherry tree and then confess the misdeed to his father. That was only a story made up years after his death to show that he was a brave and honest man. No stories are necessary, however, to show the greatness of George Washington. His devotion and courage led an army through Valley Forge and to victory in the Revolution. His honesty and loyalty helped to establish our nation.

Easter

EASTER COMES IN THE SPRING each year. It is a joyful celebration because it honors the resurrection of Christ. It is the day he is said to have risen from the dead. This happy day follows a long period of penance and mourning for the death of Jesus Christ. The 40 days, called *Lent*, begin on Ash Wednesday. They extend through Good Friday, the day of Christ's crucifixion, and end on Easter Sunday.

Easter occurs on a different Sunday each year. It is celebrated on the first Sunday that follows the first full moon after March 21st (the first day of spring). The Roman Emperor Constantine, who was a Christian, set this date for Easter back in the year 325 A.D. Most churches have followed his rule ever since.

The celebration of Easter is one of the most important holidays in Christian countries throughout the world. But many Easter customs are not religious. In America, there is an Easter "parade." In towns and cities, people go walking in their newest clothes. Men sometimes dress formally, even to a high silk hat. And women and girls must have a new Easter bonnet.

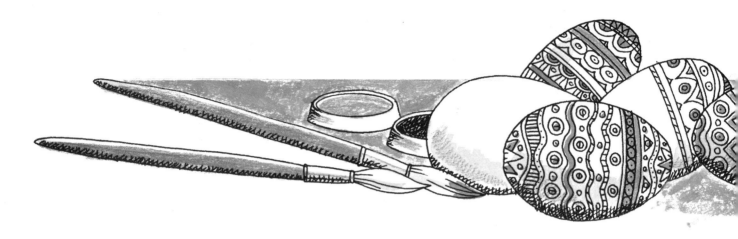

Brightly colored Easter eggs are another part of the celebration. In some areas they are given out on Easter morning. In other places, they are hidden, and children must hunt for them. Egg-rolling is another Easter pastime. Each year, an egg-rolling contest is held on the lawn of the White House in Washington. Contests are also held in England and Germany.

How did eggs come to be part of the Easter celebration? Perhaps because they are the symbol of new life. Christ's resurrection was a new life. Also, Easter comes at the beginning of spring, when all of nature comes to life after the cold winter.

The Easter rabbit appears each year, too. In Germany, people say the Easter rabbit brings the eggs and hides them in houses. This idea was brought over to the United States by German settlers.

In Russia and many of the other Slavic countries, Easter eggs are works of art. Beautiful and intricate designs of many colors are drawn on the eggs. They are painted by hand, and many are saved and passed down through the generations. The custom also includes taking the eggs to church to be blessed. In Italy, also, eggs are taken to church to be blessed.

Easter eggs, parades, and bunnies have no part at all in the Latin American Easter. All of Holy Week— the week before Easter—is a religious festival in Mexico

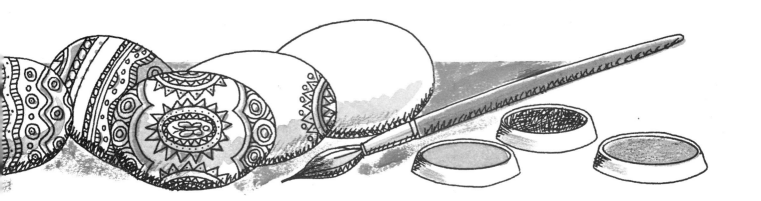

and South America. On Palm Sunday, palm leaves are blessed in the churches, as they are in many North American churches. Churches are decorated with fruit and green plants. There are religious processions and *passion plays,* telling the Easter story.

People go into deep mourning on Good Friday, but Catholics in Latin America celebrate the resurrection on Easter Saturday. After church, people go into a wild celebration, with whistles, church bells, and fireworks! In many places, people play rough games with a straw figure dressed up as Judas, who told the Roman soldiers where to capture Jesus. The Judas is hanged or burned by the crowd.

In Europe, too, there are many solemn processions on Good Friday. These are sad funeral processions mourning the death of Christ. In a town in Italy, young men run through the streets. As they run, they hit themselves on the legs with pieces of cork studded with broken glass, so that they will be hurt as Christ was.

Lent, the 40 days of penance, is an important and serious part of the Easter season. And *Carnival,* right before Lent, is the wildest holiday of the year in many parts of Europe and Latin America. There are great parades, street dances, and costume balls for three days or even longer. The biggest South American carnival is in Rio de Janeiro, Brazil. Even the very poorest people work for months to have a beautiful costume for the street dances.

French settlers brought this custom of carnival over to the United States. A *Mardi Gras* carnival is held in New Orleans each year.

Mardi Gras really means "Fat Tuesday" in French, because everyone tries to eat up the good things they will not eat after Lent begins on Ash Wednesday. In England, people often have pancake festivals. In Germany, they make doughnuts.

With all the parades and customs, though, Easter is still mainly a time to celebrate new life. Spring is in the air. The long days of winter and of Lent are over. It is a day to remember the man who was born on Christmas, died on Good Friday, and rose again on Easter Sunday.

Memorial Day

MEMORIAL DAY is the one holiday each year that is not a happy celebration. It is a special day for honoring those Americans who have died defending their country. The last Monday in May is devoted to their memory.

The United States has been through many wars—the Revolutionary War, the War of 1812, the Civil War, World Wars I and II, Korea, Vietnam. Hundreds of thousands of Americans have died on battlefields all over the world. The memory of their great sacrifice is kept alive each Memorial Day.

The custom began one year after the end of the Civil War. A group of women in Mississippi decided

to honor the graves of both Northern and Southern soldiers who had died at the battle of Shiloh in the Civil War. They decorated the graves with flowers. Two years later, in 1868, Gen. John A. Logan, commander of the Grand Army of the Republic, set aside a special day to honor those fallen in battle.

Because people placed flowers on the soldiers' graves, the day became known as Decoration Day. Even today in many parts of the United States, Memorial Day is called Decoration Day.

Today, people observe Memorial Day in much the same way as in the past. Flowers are placed on graves, and people pray for the brave men who have died. There are parades, speeches, and memorial services.

At military bases and aboard Navy ships, the flag is flown at half-mast. At noon, a memorial service is held. An honor guard stands at rigid attention while memorial services are said. A 21-gun salute and the sad notes of "Taps" played by a bugler end the ceremony.

In many ports of the United States, tiny boats filled with flowers are set afloat. From U.S. Navy ships, flowers are thrown overboard to float on the sea. These customs are to honor those who have died at sea.

At the Tomb of the Unknowns—formerly called The Tomb of the Unknown Soldier—near Washington, D.C., a ceremony is held. Buried in this tomb are men killed in World War I, World War II, and Korea. No one knows who these men were. All that is known is that they died for their country. The tomb stands to remind all Americans of the brave men who have died in battle.

Independence Day

IN THE HOT SUMMER of 1776, more than fifty men were gathered at a meeting place in Philadelphia. They were considering a document carefully written by Thomas Jefferson. It was the Declaration of Independence, the colonies' demand for their freedom.

The Revolutionary War had already begun. Paul Revere had made his famous ride to warn about the approaching British soldiers. The Minutemen had fought bravely at Concord and Lexington in Massachusetts. George Washington had been given command of the American armies fighting against the British. And Thomas Paine had called for independence and freedom in his famous essay, *Common Sense*.

The 56 men in Philadelphia represented all thirteen colonies. Such famous patriots as Benjamin Franklin, John Adams, and John Hancock were among them.

On July 4, 1776, the final version of the declaration was approved. The thirteen British colonies in America became the United States of America. All ties with England were broken. A new nation was born.

The War of Independence continued, but now there was a real cause to fight for. The cries were *liberty, freedom, independence.* Finally, in 1781, after Washington defeated Lord Cornwallis at Yorktown, Virginia, the British admitted defeat.

The first celebration of Independence Day was held in 1777, the year after the signing of the Declaration of Independence. John Adams predicted that it would be celebrated every year by all generations of Americans to follow. And he was right.

Over the years, Independence Day has been celebrated with firecrackers, sparklers, skyrockets, and roman candles. Because fireworks are dangerous, most states in the United States today restrict their use to outside displays that are carefully supervised.

Parades, marching bands, and picnics are other parts of the Fourth of July celebration. Homes display the American flag. And cities and towns are decorated with red, white, and blue bunting.

July 4th, Independence Day, is the birthday of the United States. It is a proud and important holiday. And it is a day on which we should be thankful for the wonderful freedoms demanded in the Declaration of Independence, and guaranteed by the Constitution.

Labor Day

IN 1882, A MAN NAMED Peter J. McGuire decided that there should be a holiday to honor the working-man. There were holidays, he said, to remember important patriotic, religious, and military persons. But what about the important people who work hard every day of the year? They, too, should be honored.

Peter McGuire suggested setting aside the first Monday in September each year as a holiday for the working people. He named it Labor Day. The first Monday in September was chosen because it was a pleasant time of year. Also, there was no holiday between July 4th and Thanksgiving. Most people agreed with him and thought it was a fine idea. So the first Labor Day was celebrated in 1882 in New York City.

The idea of honoring men for the work they did all year long spread quickly. In 1894, President Grover Cleveland signed a law to make the first Monday in September a national holiday.

Life was not always easy for the workingman, even in the United States. In the early 1800's men worked 12 to 15 hours a day. Women and children, too, worked long hours in factories and mines. Jobs were often dangerous. Pay was very little, barely enough for a family to live on. If a man got sick and could not work he was not paid. Some men had to work seven days a week.

After the Civil War, laborers began to organize. They wanted better working conditions and better wages. Men thought they would have a better chance as a group to face their employers. That was the beginning of *labor unions.*

The first labor union was the Knights of Labor, founded by Uriah S. Stephens in 1869. In 1886, Samuel Gompers started the American Federation of Labor (AFL). It became very large and powerful. The AFL gained higher wages and better working conditions for its members. In 1935, the Congress of Industrial Organizations (CIO) was established. In 1955, the AFL and CIO joined together.

Today, there are no longer 12-hour working days. There are good wages. Workers also get insurance, pensions, and pay when they are sick. But more important, workers have gained respect. After all, the United States grew into a great nation by the hard work of many men, who work at their jobs every day of the year.

That is why we celebrate Labor Day.

Halloween

HALLOWEEN IS THE NIGHT for ghosts and goblins, witches and black cats, haunted houses and the rattling bones of skeletons. It is the time, some say, that the headless horseman rides through the streets, his great sword flashing in the night.

Each October 31st, people almost everywhere celebrate Halloween. In the United States, children dress in costumes, They go from house to house, calling "Trick or treat." And woe to the person who cannot find some candy or cookies, an apple, or even a penny for the callers. In some places, bonfires blaze against the sky. People duck for apples. And pumpkins are carved and placed in windows to leer out at people.

Long ago many people really believed in ghosts and witches. To protect themselves and to frighten away the ghosts and witches, they built bonfires. Some wore costumes, some carried torches, and some danced around fires, hoping to scare away the "evil spirits." Many of these customs are part of our Halloween.

In England over 2,000 years ago, the Celts held a ceremony called *Samhain,* which meant "the end of the summer." The Celts believed that at Samhain the ghosts of the dead came back to earth. Bonfires were set ablaze to frighten these ghosts away. The *Druids,* who were priests of the Celts, held strange rituals. They offered human sacrifices to the gods in thanks for the harvest and for protection from the ghosts.

Many years later, the Christians continued some of the customs of Samhain, but they changed it to a different holiday. They set aside November 1st to honor all the saints in the Christian faith. They called the day All Hallows Day or All Saints Day. The evening before was All Hallows Eve, which later was shortened to simply Halloween. They celebrated this evening with bonfires, costumes, and talk of ghosts and witches.

In Ireland, they told a story about poor Jack. He was not allowed to enter heaven because he was too wicked. The devil would not have him either because Jack had played tricks on him. So, Jack was forced to wander over the earth forever, carrying a lantern.

The Irish on Halloween made "jack-o-lanterns" by carving out turnips or potatoes and placing a candle inside. Today, we carve them out of pumpkins.

In England, children beg for "soul-cakes" on Halloween. This custom began a long time ago in England, and was brought to the United States by the English settlers. In America, it was changed to "Trick or treat, money or eat." The children in England beg in different ways. Some say:

Soul! Soul! for a souling-cake!

I pray you, good missus, a souling-cake,

In another part of England, the children call:

Soul! Soul! for an apple or two!

If you have no apples,

Pears will do.

If you have no pears,

Money will do.

If you have no money,

God bless you!

Children in Scotland play a Halloween game. They go out to the fields, close their eyes and pull up a cabbage. The type of cabbage they pull is supposed to determine the kind of person they will marry. A cabbage with a close white head means an old husband. If there is dirt on the roots, the child will marry someone rich. The children then bring the cabbages home and hang them above the door.

Halloween was not celebrated much in the United States until the late 1800's. Today it is one of our favorite holidays. There are Halloween parties with prizes for the best costumes. Treats are given and sometimes tricks are played. Even though there are no ghosts or witches, it is still fun to be frightened on this one night of the year!

Thanksgiving Day

ONE OF THE FIRST really American customs was to set aside one day each year to give thanks. Everyone has something to be thankful for, be it big or small.

The day Americans have set aside to give thanks is the fourth Thursday in November—Thanksgiving Day. It is a day for family gatherings at home. Usually the feast is roast turkey, browned and juicy. There are dressing and gravy, cranberry sauce, potatoes and vegetables. And finally, there is pumpkin pie or mincemeat pie to finish off the meal.

The most important part of Thanksgiving, however, is the giving of thanks for all our blessings. That is the reason this happy holiday was started back in 1621.

The Pilgrims had arrived from England the year before. They had sailed across the ocean on the *Mayflower*, a voyage that took over two months. They had

suffered bitterly through their first winter in the New World, without warm houses or enough food to eat.

When spring came, they planted crops of corn, wheat, barley and vegetables. To get through the next winter, they had to have a good harvest. The Pilgrims worked and prayed. Finally, the harvest was in, and it was very good. The Pilgrims then set aside a day to give thanks to God.

A great feast was planned. The Pilgrims invited friendly Indians from neighboring villages. The feast included wild turkey, lobsters, clams, oysters, and venison (deer meat). The Pilgrims and the Indians feasted for three days. Unfortunately they ate up much of what they had planned to save for the coming winter. When winter came, they were often hungry.

It became the Pilgrims' custom to set aside one day each year for Thanksgiving. They did not, however, make the mistake again of not putting aside enough food to last through the winter.

George Washington called for a national day of Thanksgiving in 1789. It was to give thanks for America's success in the War of Independence. In 1863, President Abraham Lincoln set aside the last Thursday in November to be celebrated each year as Thanksgiving Day.

To observe a day of thanks is not only an American custom. In fact, it goes at least as far back as ancient Greece. The Greeks thousands of years ago had a harvest feast in honor of Demeter, their goddess of farming. The Romans had a feast for their goddess Ceres.

The Jewish people have had days of thanksgiving for thousands of years. The Feast of Tabernacles, or Booths, called *Sukkoth,* is in honor of the harvest. Little booths or baskets were made, and fruits and vegetables placed in them. Then the Jews gave thanks to God.

In many countries today, days of thanksgiving are celebrated. They are usually related to the country's day of independence, and are double celebrations.

In America, we have one day whose only purpose is to give thanks. And we have much to be thankful for.

Christmas

CHRISTMAS IS THE MOST joyful holiday of the year. On that day, December 25th, the birth of Jesus Christ is celebrated.

The birth of Christ so many years ago began a new age—the age of Christianity. His life and teachings have had more effect on the world than those of any other man in history. And on Christmas, his birthday is celebrated in every Christian country in the world.

The story of the first Christmas is perhaps the best known story ever told. Joseph, a carpenter, and his wife Mary had to return to Bethlehem for a census of all Roman citizens. Mary, who was expecting a child, rode upon a donkey. Bethlehem was crowded with

travelers, and there was no lodging to be found. It was a cold winter night. Finally, the wife of an innkeeper allowed Joseph and Mary to stay in a stable behind the inn. There Jesus Christ was born.

That night a great star was seen in the sky. Shepherds in the fields followed the star. It led them to the stable. They found Christ lying in a manger, and fell to their knees to worship the newborn king.

In Persia, three wise men, called the *Magi*, also saw the star and followed it. To them, the star was the signal for the birth of the *Messiah*, come to save the world. It was the first Christmas, quietly and sacredly celebrated in a cold and tiny stable.

Christmas is first a religious holiday. Beautiful ceremonies are held in churches everywhere to honor the birth of Jesus. The churches are decorated, and millions of people attend services.

Christmas is also a day for giving gifts and, of course, receiving them. Santa Claus, that jolly old man from the North Pole, is as much a part of Christmas as fingers are a part of your hand. They say that each Christmas Eve he loads his sleigh with toys, candy, and presents, and delivers them to all good boys and girls.

In some countries gifts are brought by St. Nicholas; in others, by Kris Kringle. The legend of Santa Claus

comes from the story of St. Nicholas, who lived over 1,600 years ago. St. Nicholas is said to have gone from house to house in those days, leaving gifts in the shoes of little children. In Belgium and Holland, it is St. Nicholas who delivers gifts. He brings them on December 6th, his feast day.

The story that Santa Claus comes down the chimney began in Norway many years ago. Our American Santa Claus, with his red suit and white beard, looks like the one in the poem "The Night Before Christmas."

The Christmas tree is another important Christmas custom. With ornaments and lights, tinsel and beads, and, of course, a star or an angel on top, it is a beautiful sight. The Christmas tree first became a part of the celebration in Germany. Some say it began with St. Boniface back in the eighth century. At that time, the Teutons, a tribe of barbarians, would sacrifice a child each year before a great oak tree. St. Boniface suggested that instead of killing a child they should cut down a fir tree, take it home and celebrate around it. Another story is that Martin Luther brought a fir tree home one Christmas Eve in the 1500's. He decorated it with candles to look like the stars in the sky.

Nativity scenes, sometimes called *cribs* or *creches*, show the Baby in the stable, with his family and the

shepherds. Homes and churches throughout the world set up manger scenes. In Bethlehem, Pennsylvania, there is the largest Nativity scene in the world. Hundreds of live animals are used, and people come from miles around to see it. The star placed above it can be seen for twenty miles.

Christmas carols are sung in the streets, in churches, and in homes at Christmas time. Holly, mistletoe, wreaths, and Christmas candles are among the most popular Christmas decorations. And, of course, there is the tradition of hanging a Christmas stocking from the mantel, to be filled by Santa Claus.

These are some ways that Christmas is celebrated in America. But in other parts of the world, there are many other Christmas customs.

In Mexico, the children play a Christmas game. A *piñata,* which is a colorfully decorated jar, is hung from the ceiling. The *piñata* is filled with gifts and candies. One child is blindfolded and given a stick. He swings the stick around in the air. When he hits the *piñata* it breaks, and the presents pour out on the floor. All the children rush to gather up the gifts. A special Mexican Christmas dish is a mixture of fruits and vegetables, covered with all kinds of candies.

The children in France do not hang up Christmas stockings. Instead, they put their shoes outside to be filled with gifts.

In Italy, each child has his own *Ceppo.* A Ceppo is shaped like a Christmas tree, except that it is made with poles and looks like a pyramid. There are shelves where gifts are placed. The bottom shelf is often a nativity scene. The Ceppo is also decorated with candles, ornaments, and pine cones.

The Yule Log is a tradition in many countries. With great ceremony the log is brought in and placed in the fireplace. People in countries as far apart as England and Yugoslavia bring in the Yule Log.

Throughout the world, children go through the streets singing Christmas carols. In Poland, carolers used to carry a star. Many dressed as shepherds and wise men. In some Slavic countries, children receive gifts as they go caroling.

Christmas dinner is always a wonderful event. It, too, is different throughout the world. In America, it is usually turkey or goose. Long ago in England, it was boar's head and brawne, peacock, and mutton pies. Some countries even serve a whole roast pig. In Poland, Christmas dinner has 12 courses. A chair at the table is always left empty in case a traveler stops.

Twelfth Night, January 6th, is an important part of some countries' Christmas celebrations. In England, it was the "twelfth day of Christmas," just as in the song. It was the day to take down the Christmas greens and burn them in a gay celebration. Some people in the United States still follow this custom.

In certain countries, January 6th, called the Day of the Three Kings, is the day of gift-giving. It is believed to be the day that the three wise men, traveling from far countries, finally arrived in Bethlehem to bring the baby Jesus their gifts of gold, frankincense, and myrrh. In Latin America, children get their gifts from the three kings on January 6th, not from Santa Claus. The three kings come riding through town, people say, and leave presents in the children's shoes set outside the door. Thoughtful children, of course, remember to leave hay and water for the kings' camels.

In South America there are exciting parades and fireworks on the Day of the Kings. People dress up as servants from Egypt and Oriental countries to march in the procession ahead of the three kings. Parades in Peru show the three kings as Ethiopian, Inca, and Spanish!

In southern France and in Spain, children go out on the eve of January 6th carrying gifts of fruit and cake for the Christ Child, and hoping to meet the three kings who will deliver their gifts. If they do not see the kings, they take their gifts to the church.

There are many Christmas customs and traditions. And all people have their own special ways of celebrating Christmas. It is a time of great joy. And it should be a time of great charity, a time of giving. After all, it is the day to celebrate the birth of Christ, who gave his life for mankind. Perhaps the best description of Christmas is in the beautiful carol:

> Silent night, Holy night,
> All is calm, all is bright.

Holidays
Throughout the World

Jewish Holidays

THE HOLIDAYS OF THE Jewish people are among the most beautiful celebrations in the world. Jewish holidays are religious, and honor important events in the history of the Jewish people.

The celebrations are held in homes and in the *synagogue*, the house of worship. Ceremonies begin at sunset on the eve of the holiday. These holidays are observed in the Jewish nation, Israel, and by Jewish people throughout the world.

Rosh Hashana is the Jewish New Year. It is a time to repent for past sins and misdeeds. In every synagogue prayers are read. A ram's horn, called a *shofar*, is blown. This is the call for people to remember their past sins and to ask forgiveness for them. At home, the people dip an apple and bread in honey. These acts call for hope in the new year. Rosh Hashana is the first day of a ten-day period of penance.

The tenth day is *Yom Kippur*, one of the holiest of all Jewish holidays. Yom Kippur is the Day of Atonement. It is a day of fasting, when people do not eat or drink. It is another day to repent for all sins. In the synagogue, services begin with the singing of a prayer, the *Kol Nidre*. The prayer begs for release from promises made to God that were not kept during the past year. At the end of Yom Kippur services, atonement for the past year is completed, and a new year begins. A candle burns in the home for the 24 hours of Yom Kippur.

One of the most festive Jewish holidays is *Purim*. It is in celebration of the deed of Esther as told in the Bible. The Book of Esther tells the story of an evil man named Haman who planned to kill all the Jews in Persia. Esther, the queen of Persia, begged the king to help the Jews. He did, and Haman was put to death. In the synagogue on Purim, the Book of Esther is read. Every time the name of Haman is mentioned, the children stamp their feet and shake noisemakers. Gifts are also given on Purim. In the past, children often dressed in costume on this day.

Hanukkah is a festival which lasts for eight days. It is sometimes called the Feast of Lights. It occurs in

December, and is a joyous occasion. Hanukkah celebrates the victory of the Maccabees over the Syrian king Antiochus. According to Jewish history, Antiochus tried to force the Jews into paganism, and to destroy the Jewish people. Led by Judas Maccabeus, the Jews defeated Antiochus. They returned to Jerusalem to rededicate their temple. The Jews found only enough sacred oil to burn for one day. Yet the oil somehow burned for eight days. Hanukkah is celebrated for eight days because of this miracle.

Each night of the eight nights of Hanukkah, a candle is lit, and prayers are said. The eight candles are held in a candelabra called a *menorah.*

Hanukkah is a time for happy celebrations. There are parties. Gifts are given. Special games are played, like the "dreidel" games. The dreidel is a spinning top with four sides. Each side has a letter of the Hebrew alphabet printed on it.

The most famous Jewish holiday is *Passover.* It celebrates the flight of the Jewish people from slavery

as told in the Bible's Book of Exodus. Led by Moses, the Jews came to the Promised Land to begin a new life of freedom.

Passover occurs in March or April each year. It lasts for eight days. Some groups of Jewish people, however, only observe seven days. The eighth day was not added until the Middle Ages.

The most important part of the Passover celebration is *Seder*. It consists of both a religious service and a meal. Special foods and wines are served. During the eight days no leavened bread — which is bread made with yeast—may be eaten. The people eat *matzoh*, an unleavened bread. On the table are symbols of Passover—a roasted lamb bone and a roasted egg.

Prayers are said and the story of Exodus is read. These are contained in a book of worship called the *Haggadah*. As part of the ceremony, the youngest child asks four questions about Passover. The questions are always the same, and the answers are contained in the Haggadah.

Passover is a special holiday for children. They take an active part in the celebrations. And it serves to remind them of the history of their people.

Moslem Holidays

PERHAPS THE LONGEST HOLIDAY in the world is the Moslem feast *Ramadan,* which lasts for a month!

Like Christians and Jews, Moslems all over the world celebrate religious holidays. They are members of the religion called *Islam,* and there are Moslems (or Mohammedans) in Pakistan, Egypt, Iran, and many other parts of Asia and Africa.

For the entire month of Ramadan, Moslems do not eat or drink during the day—but they have a wonderful feast each night. The rules for the holiday are written in the *Koran,* the Moslems' holy book. Following the rules carefully is an important part of being a good Moslem. People spend much time in the *mosque,* praying and reading the *Koran.* The last three days of Ramadan are joyous holidays when people exchange gifts, wear new clothes, and have fairs and family parties.

During the rest of the year, Moslems celebrate holidays that honor many prophets and historical figures that Christians and Jews know from the Bible.

Moslems, in fact, celebrate Adam's Birthday every Friday. They have holidays to honor Moses, Joseph, David, and Abraham, too. They believe that Abraham's second son, Ishmael, was the father of all Arabs, and that his first son, Isaac, was the father of all Jewish people. The day to honor Ishmael and Abraham is called "The Festival." People honor their dead and visit cemeteries, but they also celebrate joyously.

One holiday called *Ashura* celebrates the landing of Noah's ark. They tell the story that Noah's wife was so happy to see land that she made the best and biggest pudding in the world, with dates, raisins, figs, nuts, and currants! On Ashura, Moslem wives try to make a pudding as delicious as the one Noah's wife made.

Ashura is the last and only happy day of the long Moslem New Year, called *Muharram.* In different countries, Moslems celebrate differently—some sadly, some happily. One Moslem New Year belief is that a wonderful lotus tree is at the edge of Paradise. Each leaf bears the name of a person—one leaf for every person in the world. On the first day of the new year, they say, an angel shakes the tree. Some leaves fall. These are the people who will die during the year. So the New Year is a rather sad time. People wear black clothes, go to the mosque, and pray for the dead.

Muharram also observes another sad time—the death, or martyrdom, of Hussein, an early leader of Islam. There are plays showing the battle in which

Hussein died, and people weep and faint with grief. Sometimes they threaten the actor who plays the soldier who killed Hussein.

As Christians celebrate Christmas, the birthday of Christ, Moslems honor the *Birthday of the Prophet*, Mohammed. For nine days there are fairs, feasting, and parades. Stories are told about how the mountains danced when Mohammed was born, and sang, "There is no god but Allah." The trees answered, "And Mohammed is his Prophet." Then 7,000 angels brought a golden vase filled with heavenly dew, and his mother bathed the new baby in it. Many stories like these are told to Arab children on the Prophet's Birthday, the happiest day in the Moslem year.

European Holidays

EUROPE IS A CONTINENT with many countries. They have different languages, histories, and cultures.

Each country has its own heroes and its own special holidays. Certain holidays—Christmas and New Year's Day, for example—are celebrated by all countries in Europe. But there are certain holidays which have special meaning for just one country alone.

In France, the most important holiday of the year is Bastille Day. It is celebrated on July 14th. The Bastille was a large fortress in Paris that was used as a prison during the French Revolution. The French people were fighting for their independence, just as the people in America did during their Revolutionary War. On July 14, 1789, the French people attacked and destroyed the Bastille. Their success led to victory and freedom.

The biggest celebration is in Paris, but Bastille Day is also celebrated throughout the rest of France. Huge parades and fireworks displays are seen everywhere. Carnivals and dances sometimes last through the entire night. In Paris, there is a large torchlight parade on the eve of Bastille Day. The next morning 100 cannons are fired as a salute to the brave men who won freedom for France.

The people of France also celebrate the feast of Joan of Arc. Joan was a young maiden who led the French army against the English at the battle of Orleans in 1429. She saved France from the English. Joan, however, had made many enemies. She was later accused of being a witch, and was burned at the stake in a small

town called Rouen. Today, she is considered a martyr
and is honored all over France on her feast day.

Germany is known for its religious celebrations.
On almost all of the Christian holidays, the Germans
hold fairs, carnivals, dances, and parades.

The most famous festival is held in Munich. It is
called the Munich *Oktoberfest.* It is a carnival which
lasts for 16 days. Men and women in gay, colorful
costumes parade through the fields around Munich.
The costumes and dresses represent the clothes worn in
Germany throughout history. Horsedrawn wagons carry
food and great red casks of beer. There are games,
plays, sports, and dances.

Spain is a country where almost everyone is Roman Catholic. Their most important holidays are religious. Holy Week, the week before Easter, is the time of the biggest celebrations. Great parades are held throughout Spain. Mourners in dark hoods march to the pounding of drums. Holy images are carried through the streets, and services are held in the churches.

In the city of Seville, one of the largest and most impressive parades is held. The procession includes groups of carved statues depicting scenes from the life of Christ, carried through the streets on platforms. They are called *pasos*, and some of the statues were carved hundreds of years ago.

Spaniards also celebrate patriotic holidays. A national holiday on April 1st commemorates the end of the Spanish Civil War in 1939. And July 18th celebrates the beginning of that same war of revolution.

One of the most interesting Spanish festivals is the Run of the Bulls at Pamplona. The festival lasts from July 7th to July 14th. Bulls are turned loose in the city and charge through the streets to the Bull Ring. The men of the city run before the bulls, trying des-

perately to avoid the sharp horns of the stampeding bulls. After the bulls are in the ring, the famous Spanish bull fights are held.

Italy is another country where the most important holidays are in honor of religious events. Easter and Holy Week are a time for great processions. And many towns and villages have their own patron saint, whose feast day is a time of great celebration. In the town of Cocullo, a statue of the patron saint, Dominic, is covered with live snakes and carried in a parade.

The feast of Corpus Christi is one of the most important holidays in Italy. It occurs 60 days after Easter. The holiday is marked by beautiful processions. Young girls spread flowers in the path of the Holy Eucharist as it is carried through the streets.

In Scandinavia, people celebrate the end of the long, cold winter with spring and summer holidays. Midsummer's Eve, in June, has been celebrated for thousands of years in Sweden, Norway, Denmark, and Finland. People light huge bonfires. Gay parties go on till morning, for in midsummer, the "midnight sun" shines brightly nearly all night long.

May 1st, or *May Day*, is the traditional day to welcome spring. In Finland, trees are decorated with ribbons and streamers. Students at Uppsala University in Sweden hold a May Day race, celebrating both May Day, the end of school, and an old holiday called Walpurgis Night.

Patriotic holidays, like the birthdays of the kings and queens, are celebrated in Scandinavia. On Norway's Constitution Day, May 17th, schoolchildren march to the royal palace carrying flags. The king and prince greet the crowds of people. And the biggest Fourth of July celebration outside the United States is held in Denmark!

May Day in the Soviet Union honors workers, not springtime. It is International Labor Day, both in Russia and in other Communist nations. Crowds jam Red Square in Moscow to watch huge parades. Russians also hold huge celebrations in October and November to mark the anniversary of their Revolution in 1917.

Holidays in Great Britain

THE BRITISH ISLES include four countries — England, Ireland, Scotland and Wales. Over the years, many people from these countries have immigrated to the United States. They have brought many customs and traditions which are now part of our celebration of holidays. Yet in the British Isles they celebrate many holidays which belong only to them.

In England, the greatest celebration is the coronation of a new king or queen. This holiday may happen only once or twice within an Englishman's lifetime. But when it does occur, it is a great occasion.

The ceremonies are attended by people from all over the world. Other kings and queens, government leaders, and famous people from all walks of life come to London for the coronation. There are balls, parties, and parades. Hundreds of different uniforms are worn. Members of the House of Lords arrive in robes trimmed in ermine. Native costumes are worn by the dignitaries from other countries. And, of course, the British

46

soldiers and guards wear their brightly colored uniforms. The climax is the crowning of the new king or queen.

The birthday of the king or queen of England is also a holiday. In fact, the birthday of one of England's most famous queens, Victoria, is still celebrated each year. It is May 24th, and is called Empire Day or Commonwealth Day. In the past, an old custom for celebrating this holiday was for the English to dress in the native costume of different English colonies, like India, Australia, Canada, and even Zanzibar.

England also honors an event which never happened. Guy Fawkes Day is a holiday observed throughout England. It celebrates the "not-happening" of the Gunpowder Plot of 1605. Guy Fawkes, a treacherous villain, and his followers planned to blow up the king and Parliament. Fawkes was caught just as he was about to light the fuse on several crates of gunpowder, which were placed under the House of Lords. The plot failed and Guy Fawkes was executed the next year. On November 5th each year, the English celebrate this event which fortunately did not happen. Bonfires are set ablaze, and in many places "effigies" of Guy Fawkes are burned.

The Irish have a very special day, March 17th—St. Patrick's Day. St. Patrick is the patron saint of Ireland, even though he was not born there. St. Patrick came to Ireland in the fifth century. He brought religion to the island, and is said to have worked many miracles. The most famous story of St. Patrick is that he drove all the snakes out of Ireland. It is said that St. Patrick held up a shamrock and all the snakes fled for their lives.

St. Patrick's Day is celebrated with parades and parties. The biggest parade is held in Dublin, but parties are held everywhere.

Scotland also honors its patron saint—St. Andrew. On November 30th, his birthday is celebrated. It is a day for feasting. The traditional dish is *haggis*, which is like pudding and is cooked, of all places, in the belly of a sheep.

Young men and young women trade vows of love on the eve of St. Andrew's Day. And today, many a Scotsman celebrates this holiday with a game of golf.

But there is no disrespect for St. Andrew, because he is said to have invented the game.

The country of Wales celebrates many unusual festivals. The *Eisteddfod* is a music festival held each August. It is a very important gathering for the music-loving Welsh.

The first Eisteddfod was held in the 6th century. Mostly *bards* (poets) and minstrels, who roamed about the country in those days, attended the festival. Contests in poetry, music, and folk songs were held. Today, singers, poets, dancers and musicians from all over the country arrive. The festival formally begins with the blowing of trumpets. The music, singing, and contests begin. There is beautiful music everywhere.

Holidays in Canada

CANADA, OUR NORTHERN neighbor, has close ties with Great Britain. *Dominion Day*, July 1st, honors the day in 1867 when Canada became a nation and a member of the British Commonwealth. It is the celebration of their independence, and the festivities are much like ours of July 4th. When the weather is warm, picnics and outings are common. In the capital of Canada, Ottawa, and in the capitals of all the provinces, July 1st is a day for speeches and colorful parades.

The English who settled in Canada brought with them the celebration of *Boxing Day* on December 26th. Despite its name, the day does not honor the sport made famous by Jack Dempsey, Joe Louis, and Rocky Marciano. Instead, it is a day for giving gifts to others

who perform services during the year. To most Canadians today, Boxing Day provides a welcome rest from the excitement of Christmas Day. Originally, it was a day for the wealthy people of England to prepare "boxes" of gifts for their servants and other poor people. For people receiving "boxes," Boxing Day is Christmas, one day late!

The American holiday of Thanksgiving has traveled across the border to Canada. Each year, an official government proclamation declares a day in October which is to be set aside to give thanks for all the blessings received during the year. On the Canadian Thanksgiving, church services and a splendid turkey dinner with all the trimmings are traditional.

Latin American Holidays

FIESTA TIME! Nearly every day of the year is a holiday for some of our neighbors in Mexico and Latin America. In villages and small towns in every country, processions and parades are held to celebrate special occasions. There are religious festivals to honor many of the saints, because nearly all the people of Latin America belong to the Roman Catholic Church.

Some of these holidays are celebrated in only a few towns. Others are special occasions for people in all the many countries in South America, Central America, Mexico, and some islands in the Caribbean.

Corpus Christi Day in June is one of the most important and popular religious holidays. There are many solemn and religious parts to the celebration, and many that are not solemn or religious. "Devil dancers" roam the streets in Venezuela and Panama, shaking rattles and wearing frightening masks with horns. The idea of having parades of giants, dragons, and little devils was brought from Spain by the early settlers.

In Peru, the Corpus Christi holiday goes on for several weeks. Images or statues of favorite saints are carried into the city and are left overnight in the cathedral. The story is that once the people have left, the statues have their own festival, dancing and having fun just as ordinary people do.

Mexican children love Corpus Christi Day because they can wear special costumes. In Mexico, this holiday has become a special occasion for different kinds of workers—house builders, weavers, pottery

makers. There are miniature markets where tiny houses and tiny loaves of bread are sold, and restaurants serving tiny bites of food in what look like doll dishes. Everything is paid for with play money or pieces of candy. In other towns, though, there are parades in which everything is very big. Bakers carry huge bread loaves, and guitar makers carry guitars six feet long!

Midsummer Eve, in the middle of June, was one of the most important ancient European holidays. The Spanish and Portuguese brought this important

festival with them, and it was changed and mixed with the customs of the ancient Indians of South America. In Latin America, this holiday is called *St. John's Day*, but many customs are older than Christianity.

In many countries, people build huge bonfires to honor the sun's fire on St. John's Day. Couples dance around the bonfires. In parts of Paraguay, people walk through the live coals barefoot! In Mexico, paraders wear the feathered costumes that the Aztecs wore before the Spaniards came. They beat a huge drum and play old flutes and rattles. In other parts of Mexico, the holiday is a religious festival of John the Baptist.

Throughout all of Latin America, May 3rd is *Dia de la Cruz*, or the Day of the Holy Cross. Roadside crosses and shrines are decorated with flowers. People build special altars and crosses in their homes or gardens, and decorate them with flowers, paper decorations, statues, and ribbons.

For Mexican workmen and builders, the Day of the Holy Cross is a very special day. On the highest peak of any building being built, they erect a cross decorated with colored streamers, flags, and flowers. Firecrackers

and rockets explode all day, and sometimes small groups of musicians serenade the workers!

February 2nd, which most Americans know as Groundhog Day, is a religious holiday in many countries. It is called Candlemas or, in Spanish-speaking countries, *Candelaría*. The South American countries in the Andes Mountains, where there are many Indians, celebrate this holiday with fiestas that last for a week or more.

In the churches, candles for the coming year are blessed. Outside, in the streets and the markets, hundreds of people dance to the beat of drums. The Indian women wear many layers of bright-colored full skirts, dark shawls, and derby hats! Other dancers wear costumes—bullfighters' suits, animal skins, and costumes like the Spanish conquerors wore.

The day that we celebrate as Halloween is the beginning of a two-day religious holiday in most of Latin America. All Saints Day and All Souls Day, which come on November 1st and 2nd, honor those who have died. All Souls Day is also called "Day of the Dead," and Latin Americans make trips to cemeteries with flowers, candles, and even food. But when the solemnity is over, the Day of the Dead becomes very lively indeed, and there is dancing and a fiesta. In Mexico, it is believed that the dead need a vacation, and return to earth to take part in the celebration. So altars are built, and food is spread for these visiting "souls." Bakeries sell small sugar candies shaped like skulls, and many other toys that look like coffins or skeletons.

A special patron saint for Mexican children is San Antonio Abad. On his feast day, every child dresses up his favorite pet to be blessed by the priest in church. You might meet a cow painted with red and white stripes, a puppy wearing velvet pants and a hat, or a burro wearing a big bow tie—for pets must look their best on this special day.

Most of the Latin American countries have an "independence day" like our Fourth of July. They celebrate the birthdays of heroes like Bolivar and Juarez, as we celebrate American heroes' birthdays.

On the night of September 15th, 1821, Father Miguel Hidalgo stood on a balcony in a small Mexican town and called upon the people to rise in a revolution against the Spanish government. Independence came a year later. Now every year, his speech, called the *grito*, is repeated on that night in every city and town. In Mexico City, the President himself speaks from the National Palace. At midnight, all the bells in the cathedrals, along with factory whistles and automobile horns, welcome Independence Day, September 16th. There are parades and fireworks.

Mexicans also celebrate *Cinco de Mayo,* the Fifth of May, which is the day of a famous and important battle against the French in 1892. They stage a mock battle, with half the players dressed as famous Mexican generals and soldiers, and the others as French and Indian soldiers.

Independence Day in Peru comes on July 28th, when there are special bullfights and games. A week later, Bolivians celebrate their *Independencia* with masquerades, Indian dances, and carnivals. Rodeos are popular during Chile's independence day, September 18th. The *huaso,* Chile's cowboy, wears a broad-brimmed hat, fringed black leather leggings, and a wildly striped short cape.

Chinese Holidays

EVERY CHINESE BOY AND GIRL celebrates a birthday on the very same day of the year — the Chinese New Year. Traditionally, it is the merriest and most important holiday of the whole year. All Chinese children have other birthdays, too, of course — but part of the New Year's festival is a big birthday party.

Chinese New Year comes at the beginning of the *lunar* year (a different way of figuring time), which is usually early in February in our calendar. In the United States, many people whose families are Chinese still celebrate this holiday and January 1st too.

Chinese New Year is a 15-day holiday. People clean and paint their houses — and buy new clothes if they can.

On New Year's Day it is bad luck to step on the ground wearing old shoes!

Even before the New Year begins, Chinese families get their houses ready. The old paper image of the "Kitchen God" is given a goodbye dinner of sweet foods so he will say only sweet things about the family. Then the paper image is burned, along with bright-colored paper chariots the children have made. The "Kitchen God" travels off to heaven in a cloud of fire, and popping fireworks wish him a happy trip.

A new "Kitchen God" arrives with the New Year, and the master of the house sets up a new image, made of bright red, green, and yellow paper.

Before the New Year starts, everyone pays every penny they owe to anybody. On New Year's Eve, families seal their doors with good-luck charms and have a solemn meal to say good-bye to the old year. Children bow to their parents and wish them "Happy New Year."

The New Year ends with the Feast of Lanterns, when a huge paper dragon leads a joyful parade through the streets. As many as 100 men and boys carry the dragon—and a Chinese boy knows he is grown up when he is big enough to help carry the dragon.

Like nearly all people everywhere, the Chinese have always celebrated the arrival of spring. There are

many different spring holidays. *Li Chum*, the happiest
holiday, comes at the beginning of the spring planting
season. All the country people celebrate and pray
for good rice crops and rich harvests. In parades,
everybody carries flowers. And they honor the water
buffalo. This animal plays such a big part in farming
that he is the symbol of spring. When the people come
home from the fields, they go to traditional plays or
"plum-blossom" parties. Many go to weddings, because
Li Chum is supposed to be a lucky day to get married.

Other spring holidays also involve the growing
crops. *Yu Shui*, in late February, celebrates "spring

showers." *Ching Chi,* in March, means "The insects are stirring." Farmers run to the fields and destroy the insects who might ruin the new crops.

The Chinese have always honored their families and ancestors highly. Their "Memorial Day" is called *Ching Ming*—or the Pure and Bright Festival. They decorate cemeteries with willow twigs, and put offerings of food on their family graves. Then the living family has a picnic. Because Ching Ming is also the first real day of spring, people often plant trees on this day, too. It is a respectful holiday, but full of joy.

Japanese Holidays

JAPANESE BOYS AND GIRLS have two holidays that are especially for children.

Hina Matsuri, March 3rd, is a doll festival for girls. The family's doll collection, sometimes very old and always very beautiful, is displayed on special shelves. The emperor and empress dolls, of course, have the top shelf. Dolls dressed like court gentlemen, ladies-in-waiting, pages, and musicians sit on the lower shelves. The dolls are the hosts and hostesses for friends who visit the girls in each family. A tiny tea table is set out in front of each doll's shelf.

Doll's Day is also the Peach Blossom Festival. These flowers mean beauty and gentleness, and a branch is usually put on the shelf with the dolls.

On Boy's Day, May 5th, families who have sons fly huge paper fish on a tall pole in the garden—one for

each boy. The boys are told about the bravery and courage of their families. They are given swords or suits of armor or banners with family mottoes on them.

There are kite-flying contests and kite "battles" all during the spring and summer in Japan. One of the biggest of these kite battles is held on Boy's Day. The story of the kite-flying contests is that, hundreds of years ago, the feudal lord of Hamamatsu was so happy at the birth of his baby son that he wrote the baby's name on a huge kite so that everyone would know about it. In a five-day festival, boys of Hamamatsu battle with kites in the air. Sharp bits of glass glued to each kite string make the battle very exciting.

May 5th is also a national holiday called "Children's Day," and all Japanese children are wished happiness and prosperity.

Many Japanese holidays are religious. Since many Japanese are Buddhists, there are beautiful festivals and dances at Buddhist temples. Many other Japanese belong to the religion called *Shinto*, and have their own festivals and holidays. Still others are Christians, who observe Christmas and other Christian holidays.

Some very old holidays are nature holidays. They are held at the beginning of the rice-growing and fishing seasons and at harvest time. In one town, young girls in beautiful, old-fashioned kimonos plant the first rice seedlings, while other people chant and sing. In another town, the women rule the first days of the rice-planting. They take wooden buckets, fill them with mud from the rice paddies, and throw mud at every man they meet.

The Festival of Lanterns, or *Bon Matsuri*, is one of the biggest holidays of the year. Buddhists in Japan have celebrated it for about 1500 years.

During the Feast of Lanterns, which occurs in the middle of July, Buddhists honor members of the family who have died, including all their ancestors for thousands of years. On the first day, families take lanterns to the cemeteries to guide the spirits back to earth for the festival. Food is put on altars in the houses. On the third day, families say farewell to the spirits who have visited them. Thousands of tiny lantern-boats are set afloat on the lakes and on the ocean. Each one has a Japanese letter written on its sail.

Though Bon Matsuri honors the dead, it is not a sad time. There is dancing and singing, especially in the villages.

Japan became a democracy after World War II, and added a new holiday to its calendar — Constitution Day, May 3rd. The emperor and empress and important public officials meet in a ceremony at the entrance to the Imperial Palace in Tokyo.

Another new national holiday falls on November 23rd—it is called Labor-Thanksgiving Day. Japan has borrowed from the United States the ideas of Labor Day, when workers are honored, and Thanksgiving, when people are thankful for what they have. The Japanese have combined them into this one new holiday.

A new and solemn Japanese holiday is the *Peace Festival* held each year in Hiroshima, where the first atomic bomb was dropped in 1945. The ceremony honors those killed, and prayers are said for peace in the world. People sing songs of peace and send small lantern-boats down the river.

Holidays in India

THOUGH INDIA IS VERY OLD, it has been an independent nation for just a little over 20 years. In 1947, after being a British colony for many years, the huge country gained the right to rule itself. Today Indians celebrate Independence Day, August 15th, with pageants and parades. Republic Day, January 26th, is another patriotic holiday, marking the day India joined the British Commonwealth.

India also has many religious holidays. Its 300 million Hindus have so many festivals that two or three sometimes fall on the same day. Indian Christians, Jains, Sikhs, Moslems, and other religious groups observe their own holidays.

The Hindu festival *Divali*, "the garland of lights," is a five-in-one holiday. Five separate festivals come in a row. To get ready, Indians scrub and paint their houses and hang garlands of flowers in the doorways.

On the first night, hundreds of little oil lamps are lighted. They are hung on the walls and parapets of every house, where they will burn throughout Divali. They will light the way for Lakshmi, goddess of wealth, to visit every home. When the lamps are lit, every building is outlined with little flickering lights.

Each day of Divali honors a different Hindu god. People tell old stories about these gods and heroes. Everyone tries to have new clothes and to bathe in a flowing river, which Hindus consider holy.

The gayest and wildest of Hindu holidays is the spring festival called *Holi*. Indian boys collect all the fuel they can for the huge Holi bonfire. When the moon rises, the fires are lit. Drums boom and horns blow. Soon people are dancing around the fire singing folk songs. Crowds chase each other through the streets, throwing colored paint and yelling. At sunrise the fire is put out, and everyone marks his forehead with the ashes. Sometimes Holi goes on for more than a week, as people celebrate the coming of spring.

There are thousands of other Hindu festivals. Many honor old beliefs in the gods of the sun, moon, stars, and the spirits in plants and animals. All living things, in fact, are sacred to Hindus. Very holy men eat no meat at all, and no Hindu would kill a sacred cow. There are also millions of Hindu gods—but Hindus believe these are all different forms of one

"trinity." The gods in the trinity are *Brahma* the Creator, *Vishnu* the Preserver, and *Siva* the Destroyer.

One important holiday is the *Durga Puja,* in the autumn, which honors Siva's wife. All the houses, even very poor ones, have a statue of Durga. She is very tall, with ten arms, and rides a sacred lion. Since Durga is a mother-goddess, her holiday is also a festival for mothers. Pageants, plays, and celebrations are held the entire time, ending with a display of fireworks.

Can you imagine a day on which you honored your schoolbooks, your mother her broom, and your father his pencil or typewriter or hammer? Hindus have a Festival of Tools, to honor the god Visvakarma. Everyone puts an important tool before a pitcher that represents the god. Gardeners bring rakes. Artists bring brushes. Housewives bring brooms.

Then each person lights a candle. They give thanks for the help the tools have given them, and ask them to do good work in the coming year. Sometimes they add flowers or incense to the altar. After that, the day is a happy holiday for workers.

Parties and Entertaining

Time for a Party

PARTIES ARE A LOT OF FUN—both to give and to go to. But parties are the most fun when they are planned right. Maybe you would like to give a party for a very special occasion, but are not quite sure how. Or maybe you would just like to give a party—and need a good idea.

Many parties are for special occasions. They may be for a *birthday* or a *graduation*, for someone who is moving away, or for someone new in your school or your neighborhood. There are lots of holidays all. through the year that are also good reasons to give a party. Here is a calendar for party-giving, which you can use for your own parties, for class parties at school, or for parties that your scout troop or cub den or any other group wants to give.

Spring Parties

St. Patrick's Day (March 17) May Day (May 1)
Easter   End of School Parties
April Fool's Day (April 1)

Summer Parties

Memorial Day (May 30)   Picnics
Flag Day (June 14)   Barbecues
Independence Day (July 4)   Outdoor Parties
Labor Day (September)

Autumn Parties

Columbus Day (Oct. 12)   Hay Rides
Halloween (Oct. 31)   Hikes
Thanksgiving (November)   Square Dances

Winter Parties

Christmas (Dec. 25)   Valentine's Day (Feb. 14)
New Year's (Dec. 31 - Jan. 1) Washington's Birthday
                                 (Feb. 22)
Groundhog Day (Feb. 2)   Ice-skating or sledding
Lincoln's Birthday (Feb. 12) Caroling

How To Be a Host or Hostess

WHEN YOU DECIDE TO GIVE a party, you become someone special. You are no longer just Jack or Jane or Susan or Kevin—you are a *host* or a *hostess*.

There are certain things that you, as the host or hostess, should do.

Planning the party. Find out from your mother how many guests you may invite. Then decide which friends to ask, what time the party will be, and what kind of food to serve. Then decide if you want to have special favors or decorations. You may buy them or make them. (Pages 85-91 give you some ideas.)

Sending out invitations. Pages 72-73 show some invitations you can make yourself. If the party is to be a small one for close friends, you can telephone the invitations. Always tell *what day, what time, where,* and any special reason for the party. The guests will

want to know what kind of clothes to wear—dress-up, school clothes, play clothes, or costumes.

Greeting guests. Answer the door when guests begin to arrive, and say hello to each guest. If the guests' mothers or fathers bring them to the party, the host and hostess say hello to them, too, and ask them to come in. In cold weather, the host or hostess takes people's coats and boots and scarves and puts them away.

Introducing people. Sometimes you may invite friends from school that your mother does not know. When they arrive, you say something like, "Mother, I'd like you to meet Jane, who is in my geography class." Perhaps your friend's mother or father is at the door, too. Your friend should introduce you, just the way you would introduce your mother. But if your friend does not do this, then you introduce yourself, something like this: "I'm Sue, Mrs. Whitman. And this is my mother, Mrs. Anderson. Would you like to come in for a minute?"

Finding something for everyone to do. As the host or hostess, you start games that other people can join as they arrive. If you are very busy, you can ask a good friend to answer the door as other guests come in.

At parties for young children (preschoolers), "games" will usually be familiar songs and playing with toys. Mother, of course, will be this party's hostess. She makes certain that no one is left out of the games, and helps shy children join the fun.

But if you are older, you should be your own host or hostess as much as you can. It's *your* party and *your* friends, not your mother's!

Pages 77-83 give you some ideas for games. Probably you know many more. Maybe you and your friends enjoy other things, too, like singing songs you all know. Plan your games ahead of time, though, so that you don't have a roomful of people just sitting—or, worse yet, a roomful of boys or girls who have started to fight or yell because they don't have anything else to do.

Helping your mother at the party. You should plan with your mother what time the food will be served. When it is time, you should help her bring the food in. Make sure all the guests have been served before filling up your own plate and cup.

Saying good-bye to every guest. If mothers or fathers are calling for guests, you say hello at the door just as you did at the beginning of the party.

The host or hostess never sits and plays when guests are going home. If it is your birthday party, you should be sure to say "thank you" for your presents.

Helping to clean up. When you are the host or hostess it is your job to clear plates and cups from the table. You put away decorations, and any toys or games or records that are left out. You also pick up anything spilled on the floor—and you offer to wash the dishes.

Party Invitations

THE GUESTS WHO ARE COMING to your party need to know three important things—where it is, what time it is, and what kind of party it is.

If it is just a small party for friends you know very well, you can call them on the telephone to invite them. If it is a special party or if you are asking many guests, invitations should be sent.

You can buy invitations that have spaces for you (or your mother) to write in what your guests need to know—the time, the day, the place.

Invitations you make yourself are fun, too. You can use small cards or construction paper. For a Valentine's Day party, for instance, you could use red hearts cut out of red construction paper. For Christmas you could make snowmen, or bells, or green trees. A big orange pumpkin or black witch hat would be a good Halloween party invitation.

On written invitations, be sure to say if the guests should wear costumes or certain kinds of clothes (for a picnic or a skating party, for instance).

Sometimes you get invitations that have the letters "RSVP" or the words "Please reply" written in one corner. This means that you should call or write the person who sent the invitation and tell them whether you can go to their party. Even if these words are not on the invitation, it is much more polite to tell your host or hostess if you can come. But if the words are there, *be sure* to answer the invitation.

Party Food

HALF THE FUN OF A PARTY is eating special treats—cake and ice cream, or hot dogs and hamburgers, or whatever you like best!

Party treats are half the fun for your guests, too, so think carefully when you are planning the food and refreshments for your party. Talk over the *menu*—the food you will serve—with your mother. If you are used to helping in the kitchen, be sure to do all you can to help get the party food ready.

At many parties, especially birthdays, you may not serve a real meal. Instead, there will probably be a birthday cake with candles, and ice cream. Small, decorated paper cups with nuts or candies are nice to put at each person's plate.

If you want to have more than that, try to think of things that are both easy to make and good to eat. You can make *sandwiches* before the party starts, choosing things that both you and your friends like to eat. Peanut butter and jelly, cheese, chicken salad, and tuna salad are all good sandwiches. Nearly everyone likes hot dogs and hamburgers, but if you are having many people, be sure to ask your mother if she is willing to do all that cooking!

You and your friends probably like cakes, cookies, and ice cream. Cake and cookies are really very easy to make. For a party at Christmas time, you can make gingerbread men or cut-out cookies in the shapes of bells, trees, or a Santa Claus. For Lincoln's or Washington's birthday, you can make a "Lincoln log" or a

"cherry tree branch" from a chocolate cookie roll, made with cookie crumbs and whipped cream or ice cream.

A big, beautiful birthday cake with candles on it is one of the most exciting parts of a birthday party. But small cupcakes are fun, too, and you can decorate them for special kinds of parties. Use colored coconut and little candy eggs to make a "nest" for an Easter party. Or use pink icing and little candy hearts for a Valentine party. For Halloween, you could use orange icing and devil's food cupcakes.

Milk or soft drinks go well with cake or cookies. (Remember to have plenty in your refrigerator.) But maybe you would like something different. For summer parties, you could serve lemonade, pink lemonade, or even a tasty pink fruit punch made with pink fruit juice, lemonade, and ginger ale. For fall and winter, bright red cranberry juice, golden apple juice, or sweet cider are good. Best of all, don't forget that after a skating party or caroling there is nothing finer than hot cocoa with marshmallows floating on top!

Party Games

CHOOSING THE RIGHT KIND of party games is a very important part of making sure that everyone at a party has fun. Here are some things to think about in choosing games to play at your party.

How old are the boys and girls who will be there? This may be the most important question. For very young children, and for most preschoolers, organized games are not always possible. Perhaps the whole group will be able to play some singing games like "London Bridge" or "Farmer in the Dell," but most games should be saved for older children.

Also, some games that delight 6- and 7-year-olds may bore their 9- or 10-year-old brothers and sisters. Probably you know best what you and your friends like to do—so choose your games carefully.

Is the party to be held indoors or outdoors? In a house or an apartment? Where your party will be decides how lively and noisy the games can be. In the summer, a back yard or patio is the ideal place for all parties. If your house has a game room or family room, you have a good place for winter parties, too. But if you do not have much space—an apartment or a small house—you should plan to keep the number of guests fairly small and organize the whole party very carefully.

Check with your mother to see where you can have the party—and where the guests should not go.

Does your party have a theme—birthday, patriotic, seasonal? Many traditional and popular party games can be changed to fit the special theme of your party.

PIN THE TAIL

The oldest version of this game is "Pin the Tail on the Donkey," but the possibilities for variations are almost endless. Some are:

Pin the Hat (or Smile) on the Clown
Pin the Beard on Santa Claus
Pin the Broom on the Witch

BALLOON GAMES

Balloon Hockey: Players use brooms to sweep balloons across the other team's "goal line."

Balloon Tennis: Players keep balloons in the air using their hands. Each team uses a different color balloon, and the team that keeps its balloon up longest is the winner.

Balloon Relay: In "relay" games, the team members play one at a time. In this game, one member of each team runs up to a chair, blows up a balloon, and then breaks it by sitting on it! The team that breaks all its balloons first is the winner.

GOSSIP (TELEPHONE)

This is usually a game for girls, and can be played while guests are sitting around a table. The girl at the head of the table whispers a "message" just once to the girl next to her. That girl passes it on to her neighbor, and so on around the entire group. The one at the end repeats the message as she heard it—which is usually not at all like the first message.

TREASURE HUNT

Several peanuts, buttons, or Easter eggs (or any other small objects) are hidden around the room or the house before the party begins. Whoever finds the most during the party is the winner.

ANIMAL CHARADES

One player, or one team, chooses an animal to act out. The others must guess what he is supposed to be.

SIMON SAYS

All players sit in front of the leader, who calls out instructions: "Stand up." "Simon says sit down." "Wave your hand." "Simon says whistle."

The trick, of course, is that only when "Simon says" an order should it be followed. Players who follow an order without "Simon says" are out of the game. The player who remains in the game longest is the winner.

MUSICAL CHAIRS

You need a phonograph or piano for this game. There should be one less chair than there are players. Everyone marches or skips around the chairs while the music is playing. When it stops, everyone rushes to get a chair. The person without a chair is "out." The next time the music starts, one more chair is taken away. The game goes on until there are only two play- ers—and just one chair. The one who gets the final chair is the winner.

HOT AND COLD

While one person is out of the room, the others choose an object—a chair, someone's shoe, or anything easily seen. The person who is "It" comes back and tries to find the object. He is given clues of "You're getting warmer (or colder)" as he gets nearer to or farther away from it.

BUTTON, BUTTON

One person is "It," and stands in the center of the circle of players. All players move their hands behind their backs as if they were passing something to their neighbors, and "It" tries to guess who really has the button. He taps that person's shoulder, and if that player really has the button, he becomes "It."

CAPTAIN, MAY I

This game should be played outdoors or in a fairly large room. Players line up at a distance away from the "captain." He then gives orders to take certain steps. Any player who fails to ask "Captain, may I?" before moving must take penalty steps backwards, as the captain orders. Traditional steps include:

Giant steps—full stride.

Baby steps—one foot directly in front
  of the other, heel to toe.

Scissors steps—Jump with feet apart, then together.
When the "captain" is not looking, players can "steal" moves forward, but if he catches them they must go back to the starting line. The player who reaches the captain first is the winner.

I'M TAKING A TRIP

The first player starts off the game by saying, "I'm taking a trip to Grandmother's (or anywhere he chooses), and in my suitcase I will pack an *apple*." The second player says the whole thing again, but adds an item starting with "B": "I'm taking a trip to Grandmother's, and I will pack an *apple* and a *bicycle*." The third player adds an item beginning with "C," "I will pack an *apple*, a *bicycle*, and a *cup*." The game goes on until the alphabet is finished, or until all players give up trying to remember the list!

PENCIL AND PAPER GAMES

Word Treasure Hunts: Players are given a certain word to write at the top of their paper, and must see how many other words they can make from its letters in the time limit. Words can be appropriate to the party theme: BIRTHDAY, CHRISTMAS, REINDEER, JACK O'LANTERN, CHERRY TREE, etc.

Changing Words: By changing just one letter at a time, players try to change one short word into another word with a different meaning. "Change FLAG to a word that means a round red vegetable!"

FLAG   FLAT   FEAT   BEAT   BEET

Decorations and Costumes

TO MAKE ANY PARTY look and feel more "partyish," you can buy or make bright-colored decorations. Although many stores sell decorations, it is often more fun to make your own.

The decorations for holiday parties usually follow certain traditional ideas. Parties that are not for any special holiday can be planned around a *theme* or idea. Parties with themes are especially good for group parties—your school class or scout troop, for instance. *Costumes* can make a theme party even more fun.

Use your imagination to think up new party themes. Here are four ideas you can use—Wild West, Astronaut, Zoo or Circus, and Storybook.

Most boys and girls like to dress up as cowboys and Indians. A *Wild West* party lets everyone wear a cowboy suit or an Indian costume. Perhaps you can borrow some lipstick from your mother to draw "war paint" on your face. It is easy to make an Indian headband from paper, with a tall feather stuck in it. Wear moccasins on your feet and borrow several strings of beads from your mother or sister.

For decorations, you can try to make the room look like a corral or an Indian camp. You can roll large sheets of brown paper into a tall cone and paint it to look like a tepee.

Small round ice cream cartons can be painted to look like an Indian drum, or *tomtom*. If you make enough, you can use them as favors on the table. Make a small tepee from a paper cone for the middle of the table.

When you play games at your Wild West party, all the guests in Indian costumes can be one "team" and the "cowboys" can be the other team.

If you would rather be more modern, you can have an *Astronaut* theme for your party. For costumes, you can try to copy the suits you have seen real astronauts wearing. Or maybe you would rather invent your own space suit—one you may someday wear while exploring the planet Mars or the moon.

For table decorations, make a rocket from the cardboard tube from a roll of paper towels. (Ask your mother to save these in her kitchen.) Make a pointed nose-cone to attach to the rocket, paint it silver-gray, and stand it up in the center of the table. Cover the table with dark blue paper sprinkled with cut-out stars.

Everyone loves a *Zoo* or *Circus* party. For the Zoo party, you can dress like your favorite animals. Begin your costume with leotards or tights and a matching shirt of the right color: yellow-brown for the lion or tiger, brown for the monkey, green for the parrot, and so on. Then use paper or cloth to add a tail or ears or wings or whatever you need. You can even cut a mask out of cardboard and paint an animal face.

For a Circus party, you can use animal costumes, and add the clown, the acrobats, and the animal tamer. A pair of pajamas a few sizes too big for you is a good beginning for a clown costume. Add a ruffle around the neck, big shoes, and clown make-up on your face. Acrobats can wear tights and a shirt with spangles added. Girls can wear a bathing suit or ballet costume.

Perhaps you have a clown doll or some stuffed animals that you can use to decorate the table at a Circus or Zoo party. Long strips of red and white crepe paper can make a circus "tent" from the ceiling of the room. For favors, use animal crackers. Tie bunches of balloons to the back of each person's chair.

A *Storybook* party takes a little more work making costumes. Each guest can come as a favorite character from a story, fairy tale, or nursery rhyme. The storybook characters who arrive at this party may be just about anyone—Tom Sawyer, the Cat in the Hat, Alice in Wonderland, Old Mother Hubbard, or Pooh.

To decorate the table, you can choose almost any storybook idea, too. If you can find an old overshoe or workshoe, you can make an "Old Woman in the Shoe" centerpiece. Put as many small dolls as you can into the shoe. Or you can use stuffed dolls that look like Pooh, Piglet, the Peanuts characters, or any other storybook person.

Patriotic holidays—Washington's and Lincoln's Birthdays, Memorial Day, Independence Day call for red, white, and blue, the colors of the flag. Wide crepe paper strips can be used to make bunting around the room and a striped cloth for the table. Cardboard "firecrackers" filled with candy or popcorn make good favors and table decorations. A tiny American flag stuck in a marshmallow can sit at each person's place at the table.

Remember, though, never to drape real American flags or use them carelessly.

The log cabin theme is a good idea for *Lincoln's Birthday*, along with the red, white, and blue flag decorations, because this great president came from a family of poor pioneers.

For *Washington's Birthday*, you can use some of the stories about the first president. The "cherry tree" story is just a story, but your decorations can be small paper hatchets and little bunches of candy cherries.

Halloween parties are usually decorated in orange and black. Witches, black cats, and pumpkins are the favorite decorations. A jack-o-lantern with a big grin can be placed in the middle of the table. Since Halloween is a spooky time, you might want to keep the room dark and mysterious. Hang some of the decorations from the ceiling.

The ideas for costumes for *theme* parties can be used for Halloween costumes, too.

Christmas parties, or any other winter parties, can have snowman decorations. Use marshmallows stuck together with toothpicks to make a big snowman for the table. The table cloth can be red, white, or green crepe paper.

Christmas tree branches and holly are the other traditional Christmas decorations. Put together Christmas tree ornaments and tree branches to make small decorations for other parts of the room. You can make small green trees by cutting tree shapes from green construction paper or rolling the paper into a cone. Use crayons to decorate the trees, and make one for each guest, putting each person's name on his own tree.

For *Valentine's Day*, use red hearts cut from construction paper at each person's place. If you have a big "mailbox" for Valentines, decorate it with white paper, red hearts, and paper lace doilies.

For *Easter* parties, color Easter eggs for each person. Paint or draw their names on each egg. Use pretty colors—green, yellow, violet—to make a crepe paper table cloth. A big Easter basket filled with colored eggs and chocolate eggs is a good centerpiece. If you have a stuffed animal that looks like a rabbit, use it in the center of the table, holding candy eggs in its paws. Put green paper "straw" around it for a nest.

How To Be a Guest

DO YOU HAVE TO DO ANYTHING special when you are a guest? Don't you just go to a party and have a good time? Of course, you have a good time, but you also remember to behave so that other people at the party have a good time, too. "Party manners" do not mean that you have to sit in a corner and not do anything at all. But they do mean that you *think* about what you are doing before you do it.

Chances are that at home you are not supposed to jump on the furniture or chase your brother down the hall or scream at the top of your voice. Even if you are having a wonderful time at someone else's house, don't forget that it is someone's home, too.

When you get to a party, remember to say hello to your friend's mother or to the scout leader or to any other adult who is helping out. Remember to tell them "thank you" and "good-bye" when you leave, too. If you have never met them before, and your friends are busy somewhere else, then introduce yourself.

If you know their name, just say "Mrs. Adams, I am Joey Saunders, Bill's friend." If you don't know who they are, just tell them your own name. They will tell you their name and probably say "I'm Lucy's mother" or "I'm Tom's scoutmaster." Boys and men usually shake hands when they meet. Girls and women sometimes do.

When you are at a party, remember that you are not in charge of it. The boy or girl who is giving it is the one who decides when you will play games and when

you will eat. And they suggest the things to do. (When you give your own party, you can decide these things.)

If someone asks "What would you like to do?" you can suggest your favorite games. But if everyone else wants to play a game that you don't particularly like, be a good sport about it. Probably you *will* like the next game, so don't sulk or refuse to play. That just spoils other people's fun—and it is not one of the ways to be a good guest!

Another rule about being a good guest is "Don't be first or last." When food is served, don't rush into the dining room as if you are afraid someone will eat everything before you get there. On the other hand, don't just sit and wait to be called two or three times. If you have to leave a party early, do it quietly, not upsetting everyone else. But if the party is supposed to end at a certain time, plan to leave then.

If you have to leave a party early, tell your friend's mother: "I'm sorry but I have to leave early because my mother is picking me up at 3:00," or "I have to leave for my piano lesson," or whatever your reason is.

Did you ever hear grown-ups talk about someone "wearing out their welcome?" That is a good way to describe what happens when the last guest at a party waits and waits and doesn't get ready to go home. The people who were very glad to see you earlier now are "worn out." Maybe it is suppertime, or maybe they have other things to do. In any case, when the party is over, it is time for you to go home!

If for some reason, no one will be home at your house until later, have your mother explain this before the party. Then your host or hostess and their parents will be expecting you to stay a little later.

Sometimes you will be invited to spend the night or a weekend or an even longer time at the house of a friend or a relative. Stre-e-etch your regular party manners to cover the entire time you are a guest in someone else's house. Always check with your parents before saying yes to these invitations, so that they will know your plans and can talk them over with the other grown-ups.

When you have stayed at someone's house, it is nicest to write them a "thank-you" note, as well as saying "thank you" when you leave.

Being a good guest is not really hard at all. And the important thing to remember is that with just a little effort you can be the good guest who always gets invited to other parties. Bad guests often are not asked to come again—and so they miss many good parties!

Saying Thank You

BEFORE YOU LEAVE A PARTY, be sure to look for your friend's mother or any other adult who is in charge. Tell her "thank you" and "I had a very good time." If the party is for your friend's birthday, say "Happy Birthday" again before you leave.

Always write notes to your aunts, grandparents, and other people who send you *presents* for your birthday, Christmas, Hanukkah, or any other time. Unless you have a chance to thank them in person, you (not your mother) should write a thank-you letter. It can be very short, if you like. When writing to a friend or relative far away, it will be even nicer to say something more about how you plan to use the gift.

Here is a thank-you note like one you might write:

Dear Aunt Ruth,

Thank you very much for the red scarf you sent for my birthday. It looks very nice with my coat, and I've worn it skating several times. It's warm, too! And I think we are going to have a cold winter, because it has been snowing a lot.

Thank you again.

Love,

Jackie

When your friends or family bring presents to your birthday party, say "thank you" right then and there. Most times, you will not have to write a thank-you note for presents that you receive in person.